Animals of Africa
CHEETAHS

by Mary Meinking

FOCUS
READERS

www.focusreaders.com

Focus Readers is distributed by North Star Editions:
sales@northstareditions.com | 888-417-0195

Produced for Focus Readers by Red Line Editorial.

Photographs ©: Arnoud Quanjer/Shutterstock Images, cover, 1; WLDavies/iStockphoto, 4–5, 24 (top left); Red Line Editorial, 6; Adrio Communications Ltd/Shutterstock Images, 8; Stuart G Porter/Shutterstock Images, 10–11; Kenneth Canning/iStockphoto, 12; GP232/iStockphoto, 14–15, 16–17, 22–23; through-my-lens/iStockphoto, 18; GlobalP/iStockphoto, 20; Johan Barnard/Shutterstock Images, 24 (top right); JackF/iStockphoto, 24 (bottom left), 29; ivanmateev/iStockphoto, 24 (bottom right); Dr Ajay Kumar Singh/Shutterstock Images, 26

ISBN
978-1-63517-260-7 (hardcover)
978-1-63517-325-3 (paperback)
978-1-63517-455-7 (ebook pdf)
978-1-63517-390-1 (hosted ebook)

Library of Congress Control Number: 2017935141

Printed in the United States of America
Mankato, MN
June, 2017

About the Author

Mary Meinking works as a graphic designer during the day. In her spare time, she has written more than 30 children's books. Topics include history, arts and crafts, extreme jobs, animals, pop stars, and travel. When not working, writing, or hanging out with her family in Iowa, Mary enjoys doing crafts, photography, baking, and traveling.

TABLE OF CONTENTS

CHAPTER 1

ROAM ON THE RANGE

A cheetah looks out on the **savanna**. In the tall grass, it spots a gazelle. It lunges after the gazelle. It chases the animal at an amazing speed. Soon the cheetah has caught its meal.

A cheetah looks for its next meal.

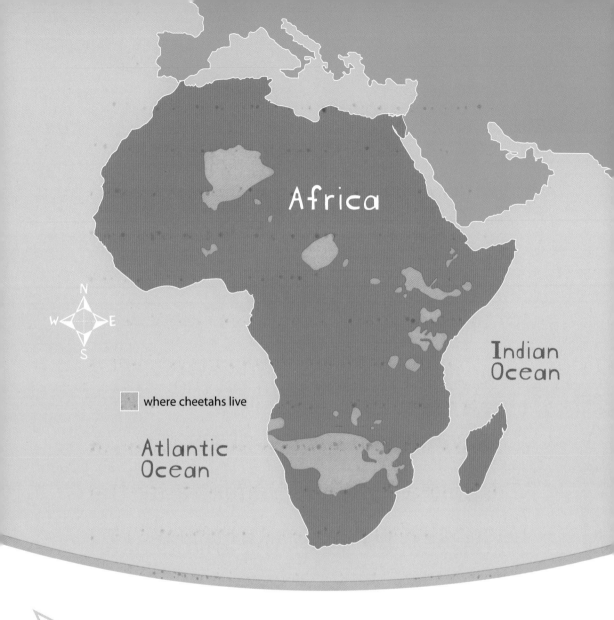

Cheetahs live in Africa.

Cheetahs make their home on the savanna. This is a dry grassland.

It is dotted with trees and shrubs. But it is mostly open plains. The plains are a perfect place for cheetahs to hunt. They have plenty of space to run down their **prey**. Sometimes it is hard for cheetahs to see great distances on the plains. So cheetahs climb trees or termite mounds to spot their next meal.

FUN FACT

Cheetahs are the world's fastest land animals.

Sometimes cheetahs climb trees to look for prey.

To survive, cheetahs need to roam. They look for food, water, and cover. Cheetahs have **territories**. Female cheetahs live alone. Each female's range is approximately 345 square miles (894 sq. km). Sometimes their territories overlap. Male cheetahs live in groups. Their territories are smaller. They are usually 5 to 10 square miles (13 to 26 sq. km). But they can be much larger.

CHAPTER 2

SPOTTED SPRINTER

Cheetahs have tan fur. It is covered in black spots. Each cheetah's coat has a different pattern. They have black marks that run from their eyes to their mouths. The markings look like tears.

 Black markings under a cheetah's eyes help it hunt in bright sunlight.

 A cheetah's tail can be up to 33 inches (84 cm) long.

Cheetahs are medium-sized cats. They weigh between 84 and 143 pounds (38 and 65 kg). Male cheetahs are larger than females.

A cheetah has a thin body. Its legs are long and powerful.

Its head is small and round. The eyes are high on the animal's head. The cheetah's ears are wide and round.

A cheetah has a long tail. It is half as long as the animal's body. But a cheetah's tail is not round and puffy like most cats' tails. Its tail is flat.

FUN FACT

Cheetahs have good eyesight. They can see prey up to 2 miles (3.2 km) away. They see as well as a human using binoculars.

CHIRP INSTEAD OF ROAR

Many big cats roar. But cheetahs cannot. The inside of a cheetah's throat is more similar to a house cat's throat. Instead of roaring, cheetahs use eight different calls.

They can purr, hiss, and growl. They also chirr, meow, and howl. They even gurgle and chirp. The chirp sounds similar to a bird.

Each call has a purpose. Some are used to call **cubs** or mates. Cheetahs use different calls when they are relaxed or in a fight.

A cheetah growls and bares its sharp teeth.

CHAPTER 3

BUILT FOR SPEED

A cheetah's body is built for speed. The animal has loose **joints** in its shoulders and hips. This allows the cheetah's legs to stretch out as far as possible. Its flexible spine can change shape with each stride.

A cheetah arches its back.

 A cheetah's long tail is striped at the end.

A cheetah can reach speeds of 61 miles per hour (98 km/h) in seconds. The cheetah's speed helps the animal chase down its prey. A long tail helps the cheetah balance as it twists and turns while running. A cheetah's tail works like a rudder on a boat. It pushes the air to change the cheetah's direction. But a cheetah cannot run long distances after prey. They usually run fast for only a little while.

PARTS OF A CHEETAH

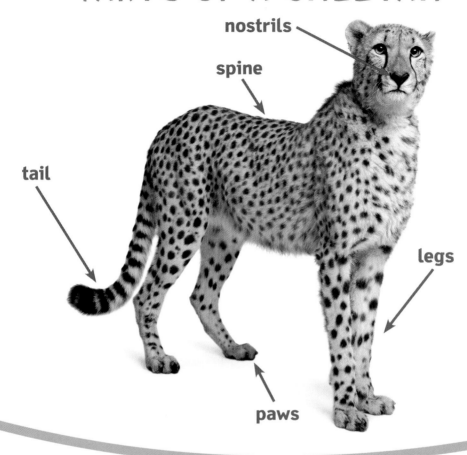

nostrils

spine

tail

legs

paws

A cheetah's paw pads are hard. Its claws cannot **retract**. This makes the paws work like soccer cleats. The paws give cheetahs great traction. They can grip the ground as the cheetah runs.

A cheetah has large nostrils and lungs. This means oxygen can enter the animal's body quickly. A cheetah also has a large heart. It pumps a lot of blood. This helps the cheetah run fast.

FUN FACT

Running fast takes a lot of energy. After catching prey, cheetahs must rest for a while before eating.

CHAPTER 4

FAST FOOD

A female cheetah has three to five cubs at a time. Cubs are born blind. The mother finds places to hide her **litter**. She moves them often. She does this so **predators** will not harm the cubs.

A mother moves her cub to a new hiding place.

CHEETAH LIFE CYCLE

Mothers have a litter of cubs.

At two years old, females leave their litter. They live and hunt alone.

Males live and hunt together.

Wild cheetahs live 8 to 10 years.

Cheetah cubs begin eating meat when they are three to five months old. Later, cubs begin stalking prey. The mother cheetah brings prey to her cubs to practice sneaking up on it.

When the cubs are approximately 18 months old, their mother leaves them. But the cubs stay together to practice hunting for several months. Later, females leave to live on their own. Males stay together for life. They form a **coalition**.

 **Water buffalo are sometimes food for cheetahs.**

Cheetahs are **carnivores**. They often hunt gazelles. Cheetahs also eat hares, birds, and young antelopes. They might eat zebras and warthogs, too. Male coalitions hunt as a group. This lets them bring down bigger prey. Female cheetahs hunt alone. They hunt small prey. A female uses its speed to approach prey from behind. Then it trips the prey by swiping at its hind feet. The cheetah quickly bites the prey's neck.

FUN FACT

Cheetahs hunt in the early morning and late afternoon. They rest the remainder of the day. They wait for prey to come near them.

FOCUS ON
CHEETAHS

Write your answers on a separate sheet of paper.

1. Write a sentence that describes the main ideas from Chapter 3.

2. Would you like to see a cheetah run? Why or why not?

3. How do cheetahs sometimes spot their meals?
   A. They look underground.
   B. They run for hours.
   C. They climb trees.

4. Why don't adult males and females hunt together?
   A. because the males do not share food
   B. because the females are not carnivores
   C. because males and females live separately

5. What does **traction** mean in this book?

*The paws give cheetahs great **traction**. They can grip the ground as the cheetah runs.*

    A. the distance an animal runs
    B. the ability to hold on to a surface
    C. the sharpness of a claw

6. What does **stalking** mean in this book?

*Later, cubs begin **stalking** prey. The mother cheetah brings prey to her cubs to practice sneaking up on it.*

    A. hunting slowly and quietly
    B. eating quickly
    C. peeling off the skin

Answer key on page 32.

GLOSSARY

carnivores
Flesh-eating animals.

coalition
A group of male cheetahs.

cubs
Young meat-eating animals.

joints
Parts of the body where two bones meet.

litter
A group of animals born to the same mother at the same time.

predators
Animals that hunt other animals for food.

prey
An animal that is hunted and killed by another animal for food.

retract
To pull in one's claws.

savanna
A grassland with few or no trees.

territories
Areas that are defended by a group of animals.

TO LEARN MORE

BOOKS

Higgins, Melissa. *Grassland Ecosystems*. Minneapolis: Abdo Publishing, 2016.

Morgan, Sally. *Cheetahs*. Irvine, CA: QEB Publishing, 2014.

Murray, Julie. *Cheetahs*. Minneapolis: Abdo Publishing, 2012.

NOTE TO EDUCATORS

Visit **www.focusreaders.com** to find lesson plans, activities, links, and other resources related to this title.

INDEX

Answer Key: 1. Answers will vary; **2.** Answers will vary; **3.** C; **4.** C; **5.** B; **6.** A